"Checchino"
Francesco Battisti

CHECCHINO

A FATHER & SON JOURNEY TOWARD DUSK

by
Francis L. Battisti

with
Suzanne Meredith

Published by
J.E.T. Creative Media
265 Main Street
Binghamton NewYork, 13905

Designed by Robert J. Gomulka.
Edited by Angelo Zuccolo.
Contributing Author, Suzanne Meredith.

Manufactured in the United States of America.

Attention: Schools and Businesses

J.E.T. Creative Media books are available at quantity discounts with
bulk purchase for educational, business, or sales promotional use.
For information, please write to:
J.E.T. Creative Media, 265 Main Street, Binghamton, New York 13905

DEDICATION

To All Who Have Come
Before Me - Enlightening the Path for the Journey

To the Generations of Family Members
Whom I Have Met Through Our Shared
Ancestry and Through Our Mutual Thoughts

To My Students and Academic Colleagues
Who Allow Me to Think, Create, and Explore

To My Clients
Who Allow Me the Privilege
of Entering Their Inner Worlds
The Sacred Ground

To My Friends and Acquaintances
For the Guidance, Camaraderie and Laughter
Over These Many Years

To My Beloved Brother, Maurice and Sister, Donamari
And their Spouses, Dianne and Ron
Who Have Accepted Me As I Am

To My Nurturing Parents
Frank and Sylvia
For Creating a Loving, Nurturing Foundation
Called Home

To My Sons
Paul, Brian, Christopher
For Bestowing on Me the Title of Dad

To My Life-long Beautiful Partner
Helen
For Being, Sharing and Loving

To God

Thank You!

INTRODUCTIONS

by

Paul - Brian - Christopher - Helen
Battisti

Three young men, whose lives were forever changed by the love and loss of their grandfather...Francesco Battisti...join with his loving daughter-in-law Helen...to pen a tribute of memories to introduce... <u>Checchino</u>.

When times are tough, I talk to him. When I need that extra help, I pray to him. When I am lost, I look to him.

Although my grandpa has been dead for over five years I still talk to him, just as I did when he was alive. At the age of 16, I knew Grandpa was my best friend. This is definitely not something many people can say and the thought still fills me with pride.

A man of great strength, both physically and mentally, Frank Battisti was quoted many times, "When I walk, I make the ground shake." He was a man of tremendous power tempered with incredible elegance.

I remember sitting on his lap as a child and listening to captivating stories of his life in the "Old Country".

As Grandpa began to physically deteriorate, he maintained a mental stability and a sharp mind right to the end.

Part of me wanted to break down in tears when I saw

him struggle to get up from a chair or painfully use a walker or have difficulty dressing. However, a great feeling of joy coursed through my body when I was able to assist him with these tasks…just as he did these things for me throughout my childhood.

I miss Grandpa immensely and he is continually in my thoughts. He is still the first and last person I speak to every day. Although he is no longer here physically, his spirit will live in me forever.

Grandpa, I love you.

Paul

In 1998 I started college and moved away from home. I was there only intermittently after Grandpa came to spend the last year of his life with us. I remember vividly each time I returned home to find him a little weaker physically. Mentally he never seemed to falter. He never lost a sense of humor and remained devilish, quick with a joke and sly as a fox to the very end.

Toward the last days, I noticed he seemed to be at peace with what was going to happen, although he never admitted defeat. He had beaten cancer once and now had the strength to stand up and accept the inevitable. His pride deepened as he allowed my father and brothers to care for him…and accepted this with great dignity.

I often wonder if I have the strength my grandpa exhibited…and I hope I do. This deep strength is not something you find at the gym or win in a fight, but rather it is what you are…strong in heart and faith.

Brian

My grandpa lived with us for a time before he passed away and the experience made me a stronger person. I saw a man in great pain who never complained or made problems for anyone else.

There are times when you hear stories about a person, but the reality falls far short when you actually meet. I heard tales about how tough Grandpa's life was when he came to the United States and how he worked hard and earned everything the family owned.

Every day he maintained a strong and tough image. Although by the time he died he weighed a little over 100 pounds, the only way I remember him is with the strength he maintained before cancer claimed his body.

The time he spent living with us makes me feel as though he is not gone, just away, in a place where I can't see him. I still talk to him as though we are having a conversation. Cancer ended his life but it did not defeat him. From him I learned that both fear and fate must be faced…and that while a person lives it is never too late.

During his last year on earth, Grandpa reunited his two

sons, my dad and uncle Maurice. He rekindled the feeling of family, of brotherhood.

While he was lying on his deathbed and supposedly non-responsive, I would put my finger in his hand and talk to him. As I talked I could feel his hand gently squeeze my finger. He may have been down, but never out.

Grandpa and I became closer when he lived with us. I helped with everyday tasks such as hygiene and trips to the bathroom; but I never felt weird or uncomfortable. He had a way to make us all feel calm in a difficult situation.

Whenever I want to stop, or feel that I can't keep going, I think of him…he never quit. I am of his blood and perhaps I do have more of him in me than I ever imagined.

Christopher

My mother died in January, 1999. It was the same year we lost my father-in-law, Frank. Of my three siblings I was the closest in proximity and also the executor of Mother's will. She died of pancreatic cancer. We all knew she was dying, and we spent the final ten months of her life talking, saying all the things we wanted to say and doing all the things we wanted to do.

My mother and I sat one afternoon, about a week before she died, and we wrote her obituary together. She taught me how to die with dignity, and gave me the opportunity to walk with her to heaven's door.

Two months later I was involved in a major motor vehicle accident which left me incapacitated for a number of weeks.

It was during this time that Frank's health turned and we began his final journey.

Unfortunately, and yet fortunately, I was exhausted both mentally and physically. Looking back after Frank's death, I realized how important it had been for me, as a woman, to be absent from his day to day care. For in the absence of a female, we were all privileged to witness the power of male caregiving.

Helen

In the sunset of my father's life he allowed me to accompany him...to be his caregiver. Through this journey we "real men" were able to share emotions and relate to each other during a transition from father and son to companions on "Checchino's" final mile to eternity. However, it was a challenge just reaching the point where Dad and I were comfortable with this evolution in our relationship.

When I was young I could not imagine a time when Dad and I could relate as equals. For most of my life he was tough, unbending, often ornery...and Dad and I butted heads regularly.

Thank God for the time factor, because as the years went on he did indeed become more approachable, more mellow, and our lives became more balanced. Perhaps, I too learned with age to relax and appreciate this good man.

It may have been Dad's early life experiences that made him so determinedly dominant. He was born Francesco Battisti in Italy in 1914 to a family of seven children. His father, Mauricio, went to the United States early in Francesco's life...and stayed for several years earning money to send back to the family in Italy.

In the old country, Dad grew up with his grandfather as a role model...a closeness developed between them that had a lifelong effect on Dad. A lingering reminder of his grandfather and his sister in Italy was a fond nickname, given to young Francesco, "Checchino"...pronounced "Keck-ino". After living in America for many years the name was still used by his brothers and sister. At one point it occurred to me to ask the meaning of the name. Dad said it was "Frank", but after repeated questions I learned it was

"Little Frank" or "young one". The Italian word holds such character that I came to associate it with my father.

In 1929, my grandfather Mauricio, sent passage costs for Checcino. He would be joining two of his brothers who had immigrated to the United States a year before. Mauricio intended to give his oldest sons American opportunities and to remove them from the influence of Fascism.

Benito Mussolini, the dictator of Italy from the early 1920's to his death in 1945, demanded homage from even the youngest citizen and indoctrination had already begun for the Battisti boys. The children had been "required" to march in parades in honor of "Il Duce".

As Dad readied for the great ocean voyage, his grandfather imparted advice to guide him: "…eventually, when you are 25, marry a good woman, make sure she is Italian and always maintain your good reputation." My great-grandfather lived through some of the most traumatic eras in the history of the world but he never saw these three grandsons again.

"An honest man is the noblest work of God."

—Alexander Pope

Years later Checchino would advise his own three children, "Be honest, if you lose your good name you lose everything." I think all of us learned integrity from Dad... to be honest to yourself and to life...take responsibility for the decisions of today because they create our tomorrows... to follow your passions in finding your own purpose in life.

My remembrances of Dad often lead to the rich legacy he gave his family...teachings...or principles...that were his own basic insights. The following thoughts from Dad have contributed to my own satisfaction with life:

See beyond the visible, trust your instincts.

Relish the moment. Some people just go through the motions of living...but everything you do is important somewhere down the line; absorb each second of life. The cycle of life ignites living...tremble with the energy and excitement of existence.

Learning creates...Get a good education... learning should never end.

Family is community.

Maintain your dignity.

Life is always in change, accept this reality.

Honesty, integrity, morality are necessary for personal contentment.

The New World Beckons

"A hazard of new fortunes….."
—*Shakespeare*

As the second decade of the twentieth century was ending, Dad traveled to the new world alone, as a third class passenger on an ocean liner, sharing a room with strangers. The trip to New York took 8 days on the high seas.

Maurico Battisti met his young son at the dock when he arrived in New York, so Francesco did not have to be processed through Ellis Island. When Dad touched United States soil, he kissed the ground, shouting; "God Bless America." For his entire life he was proud to be an American and at the same time also fiercely possessive of his Italian heritage.

After living together for a year in Ithaca, New York, Maurico returned to Italy…leaving the boys to make their own way in the world. From this point on, Dad was virtually an orphan.

I believe the experience left a longing in Dad to establish his own home and family. Although he was somewhat angry at his father's desertion again, Frank, at 14, already considered himself a man.

This experience is probably the reason Dad was conservative about giving his trust…always advising, "Don't hurt others, but make sure they don't hurt you. Be on guard."

Work Hard

"Every man's work shall be made manifest."
—I Corinthians. 3

Dad's first job in the United States was working in a Greek restaurant. He diligently learned the language of the owners and was quite adept at speaking Greek before finding out the words were not the English he thought he was mastering. Dad remained employed at this restaurant until 1933 when he joined the Civilian Conservation Corps.

Black Thursday and the stock market crash of 1929 precipitated the Great Depression. By 1933 the destroyed economy had put more than 13 million people out of work. The newly elected president of the United States, Franklin D. Roosevelt, created one of the most efficient relief programs ever instituted by the federal government: The Civilian Conservation Corps (CCC). Dad became part of this history-making project.

Years later, Dad told stories of that time saying the nine months he spent in the CCC were some of the best of his life. During his stay in the Corps, while stationed in Boise, Idaho, he became a master sergeant and worked in the mess hall cooking for large groups of fellow workers.

The first day he reported to the CCC he was told he would be on KP duty. His pride inflated when he learned that KP meant Kitchen Police. He arrived at the kitchen looking to put things in order as a police officer. However, the reality set in when he was ordered to peel thousands of potatoes.

With great pride Dad sent his parents in Italy a photo of himself in the CCC uniform...receiving a blistering reply in return. His father maintained his sons were saved from Italian military duty by bringing them to America and now Frank was voluntarily serving in the uniform of another country.

Dad's sense of responsibility led to many years of sending money to the family in Italy, despite the occasional misunderstandings.

"Knowledge...Learning Equals Creativity."

—Dad

Dad also spent time working in Ithaca on the Cornell University campus, again acquiring knowledge about cooking while on the job. As a maintenance worker he scheduled his duties to coincide with the cooking classes in the campus restaurant. He absorbed information as he swept the floors. Dad told us his learning came through the "back door" of Cornell. "You kids will go through the front door for an education."

Checchino's father thought an education would buy him nothing and discouraged any interest in schooling. All three of us, my brother Maurice, my sister Donamari and I, fulfilled Dad's prophesy and went to college. He gladly shouldered this financial responsibility to make life better for following generations.

Checchino eventually moved to Endicott and worked first in a restaurant, then at the great Endicott-Johnson Shoe Corporation. In the process of finding a good job he also found his "good Italian woman." On their first date he proposed. Two years later, Sylvia Morlando became Mrs. Battisti on Frank's 25th birthday.

In those days EJ was the best place in the twin river valley to work. Dad often commented that it was like a home for foreigners. People from all over Europe found steady employment in a "company town" that really seemed to care about the comfort of its workers.

"There's No Place Like Home."
—Dorothy - The Wizard of Oz

Owning his own home was a need for Dad…as a base for "family"…a place to belong. Mom was always the heart and soul of the family. Acknowledging that Dad was the head of the household, she claimed to be the strong neck that guided the head. His word was law but Mom was the power behind the "man of the house".

Holidays at home were special occasions throughout our lives. Mom would bake a many-layered cake and prepare the mandatory large Italian meal. Love was measured by how much you ingested at these festivities. The mantra was "Mangia, Mangia!" (Eat! Eat!)

Our house was constructed by my mother's father, who was a builder. The home was a haven for Dad, and another source of pride. He never wanted to take vacations… he was always happiest at home and thought we should all share his view. His obstinate opinion about no travel caused distress for the rest of the family. All of us would have loved to see more of the country…but Dad was boss.

Later, after all the children were grown, this too changed. My parents would travel sometimes, often to visit relatives. Eventually a trip to Europe occurred, and then one to Hawaii.

Dad's deep regard for the family house has been passed down to his descendants. My sons own the home now and, because of love for their grandfather, they have even kept the same phone number. The house anchors their roots and memories and I'm not sure they will ever want to sell it.

"Don't spend energy worrying about the unjust opinions of others."

—Dad

After marriage, Dad continued to work at the EJ shoe factory for 36 years, while also developing a part-time catering business. At the shoe factory, doing piece work, he earned $35.00 a week….and a lot more money from catering.

The extra income made it possible for Dad to indulge in his image of success…a new car. Mom added to the economic comfort level by assisting in the catering business, selling Avon beauty products and renting the upstairs of our house to tenants, usually to International Business Machine students.

Envious co-workers sniggered that the Battisti prosperity was probably due to being "connected" with Italian gangsters…not wanting to acknowledge that hard work by the whole family was responsible.

The "Mob" actually did have a strong presence in the area but Dad made a point of never developing "a relationship" with them. All the local Mafia "Godfathers" were well-known and Dad was strict about who his children associated with…steering us away from friendships with certain families. As usual, I was the most vocal in my disagreement with these dictates…always "pushing the envelope"… always wanting more freedom from Dad's dictates.

By this time our family consisted of three healthy children…, an older brother, a younger sister, and I. Mom lost two babies close to birth and carried a sadness in her heart that those children had to be buried alone in ground that had not been consecrated. Neither child had lived long enough to be baptized.

"Cherish life and all the time in that life.
Relish the moment...be alive."

—S. Rose

From the stories I heard about the day I was born, it should have been an indication of what my future would be with Dad.

It was a cold day in January and Mom had a bad complication in her pregnancy...toxemia. Because of the medical danger, she was in the hospital for several days before and after my birth.

At one point the doctor tried to discuss the problems with Dad and asked him what his choice would be...if it came to a choice...between saving the life of the baby or the wife. Dad did not hesitate to forcefully tell the doctor, "Doc, two went into that room and two better come out alive or you don't come out!"

Dad would not bargain with fate...or with the medical profession.

As the years passed it was a big occasion when Dad phoned his parents in Italy. In those days the connection to foreign shores took almost a whole day to arrange. After the conversation, he was both happy and melancholy. There was often talk about visiting Italy and seeing the many relatives still in the home town, but none of the three brothers returned while their parents were alive.

When Dad's father died I remember vividly the telephone call...and Dad's tears. It was a shock to see the degree of grief displayed by my "strong Italian parent". I had never before seen the "real man" cry. He was always a tough person because life had called that trait forth, but he also possessed deep feelings and emotions.

A few months later, this poignant upheaval was repeated when his mother passed away. It was, perhaps, the first time the mortality of parents became obvious to me. I found the awareness was a bit daunting...my own mom and dad had less time ahead of them than behind.

"Reality is the shadow of dreams."
—X. Fox

Growing up in the 1950's as an all American boy, my heroes, for a time, were John Wayne, Superman, and Mickey Mantle. They personified my ideas of an "ideal man"…short on emotion, long on aggression. They fought and won every war…on the front and at home. These were the ideals by which I measured my father.

It seemed that most of my friends had fathers who had served in World War II or in the Korean conflict…and each of them had almost single-handedly won it. These same fathers could also do everything mechanical, tune up cars and build great basement bomb shelters that even President Eisenhower would have admired.

All those fathers also spoke distinctly, being several generations removed from Ellis Island. Most noticeable, all of them could throw a baseball and use a bat with a precision fit for the major leagues. Such are the perceptions of youth.

I had been short-changed! Dad didn't serve in any war and was never in the military…only something called the CCC. Talking about that experience he would pronounce it the Civilian Conservation Corps…emphasis on the corps. As I got older, I would laugh mockingly at his old world phrases and accent…behavior that is now painful to remember.

Dad's total mechanical ability consisted of being able to light the gas stoves in restaurants and church halls where he catered meals. He was a cook...women's work, not something you would ever catch John Wayne doing. In fact, if memory serves correct, old John spent all his time in wars, roping cows, saving women and the world...but the guy never ate at all.

Superman never had an accent, but, when my dad spoke, people sometimes needed a little clarification. Superman flew through the air and repelled bullets. In the 1950's, before the era of political correctness, an accent was just not acceptable for a good guy.

Also, Dad did not catch, hit, bowl, run, golf, or even cheer. Dad just wasn't interested enough to be involved in sports...but there was a reason.

Many years later I heard him tell a story about an incident that occurred when he was 14 years old. He was taking a walk in Ithaca shortly after arriving from Italy. As he was passing a school, a football flew over the school fence almost into his arms. He picked the ball up and kicked it back over the fence and beyond where the football team was practicing.

The amazed coach raced after the kid who could kick with such precision and wanted to meet Dad's father...and gain a recruit for his team. Not understanding the situation, the non-English-speaking boy ran away. However, someone recognized him and gave his name to the coach.

That evening the coach visited Dad and his father, explaining why he was interested in the young Frank. Could he attend the local school? Was he interested in playing football? The squad did not have a kicker and this foreign-born soccer player was just what the team needed.

Dad was excited that he might be able to return to school and "make something" of himself. To be educated in America was a dream come true. However, Checchino's father believed an education would get him nowhere... claiming he should learn a trade as a way to support himself... also...sports were a frivolous waste of time that provided no return...so the dream ended.

As the years of my childhood began to pass, I realized that John Wayne was just an actor and Superman was only a cartoon on colorful pages. Neither would leave me a legacy to follow. And Mickey Mantle? Well, he had his own demons to work on.

Dad was a genuine man, a dreamer perhaps, but a man who believed that work, emotion, honesty and perseverance were the qualities that make a "real man". And so I learned...and still learn.

"Be present in every second of your existence...for the experience in these moments reflects throughout your future."

—*Anonymous*

A fond memory of my early childhood was waiting for Dad to arrive home from work...smelling of leather from cutting soles all day in the shoe factory. He would meet us in the kitchen...the heart of our home...and immediately want a cup of coffee.

With the grace of an artist he would sit in "his" chair at the table...place two teaspoons of sugar into the cup and stir it delicately...making the magic brew his own. Many times a dollop of anisette found its way into the coffee. Mom would be making dinner and Dad would unwind by telling "Se" (his nickname for Sylvia) what had transpired during the day.

Some of Dad's stories revolved around his friend "Bafeet". Italians love to christen friends with new names. When you are baptized with a nickname it means you become part of the extended family. Bafeet was older than Dad and a person he respected...a status not lightly granted.

He always spoke highly of Bafeet, often recounting his friend's great love of fishing. Spending a leisurely retirement near the water, with a pole in hand, was a goal Bafeet dreamed about...counting the years...months... hours...until that golden time.

One day Dad arrived home, sat at the table...and just sat...no coffee...no talk. He hesitatingly told us that Bafeet had a heart attack the previous evening and died.

I never forgot the principle learned from this story...we need to move forward each day. Don't wait for the great moments...each minute is important...don't put off finding the time to be true to your spirit. Spend moments with friends and in pursuit of interests you love. Work and joy should reside in the same heart...at the same time.

The Rock Garden

Dad was a firm taskmaster as we were growing up. His word was law, and he did not believe in leisure time. Any spare moment, especially Saturdays, his children were set to work at picking rocks from the garden.

My sister, Donamari, and I would rather have played with our buddies but the orders were firm….. "No play, rocks, now!" My rift with Dad widened as I expressed my opinion of his strictness. I wanted to have more fun.

The rock picking may sound like an innocent chore, but if you have never been assigned this prestigious duty, you have no idea what it entails. Your work disposing of stones is never done. Nature has a way of regenerating those rocks and they reappear back in the garden each year…sometimes propagating weekly! I am sure Endicott rocks were the inspiration for the prolific Star Trek tribbles.

The "Knob" in Endicott (an ethnic designation meaning the Italian section) was famous for back yard gardens. We lived just a few streets away from this area. Dad thought it seemed more American and more progressive to live here…in the house Mom's father built.

But we were close enough to the heavily populated Italian streets for Dad to engage in garden competition… and he loved his garden. Each man tried to outdo neighbors and relatives in a race to grow the most and best produce in the smallest space.

In retrospect, I see that the garden was a way for Dad to provide for his family, stay in good physical shape, and enjoy the outdoors.

Dad's absolute "iron man" policy of "work and work harder" caused the usual simmer of youthful emotions, but in the end we did what was expected of us. This same attitude about everything probably also caused a respectful distance at times. He was a man I deeply loved but I was not sure I always liked him. It was many years later before Dad and I became close as adult men.

The diligent example Dad set with regard to a work ethic is probably responsible for my position today. I enjoy, perhaps even love, my work as an educator. It allows me the opportunity to meet individuals at various levels of their experience and growth.

From workshops, academic course work, management training and psychotherapy...individuals and organizations allow me into their personal and intimate lives to assist with their transformation and growth. This is my garden.

"Wisdom comes only when you stop looking for it and start living the life the Creator intended for you."

—Native American Proverb

Through the years, I continued to challenge the alpha male of our household. A good example of this was an event when I graduated from college. I was the first person in the family to achieve a degree.

Education was so important to Dad that he offered to give me the cash to purchase a car...and I could pay him back over time. Wow...my own vehicle. Any kind of car I wanted? I looked at the best and decided on a Corvette... what a car! What a statement!

I announced to Dad that the car I wanted would cost $6,400. Dad did not know cars but the amount caused him to loudly inquire... "What...is this a Cadillac? Did you talk him down? What did I send you to college for if you don't bargain for a car?" He looked at the vehicle and with shock inquired... "What! Where is the rest of the car?" It was, naturally, a 2-seat sports car...not what he was expecting to pay for.

More of the same conversation ensued and it was decided that the car salesman would talk to Dad in person. When the man arrived at the family restaurant Dad made him an offer. "Take $5,400 cash and we got a deal." The man compromised and said a deal would be $5,800...Dad indignantly, in his broken English, demanded, "What's the matter, don't you understand the language...only $5,400.!!"... and then ordered the salesman to leave the restaurant. Two days later the dealer agreed to $5,400. Then Dad found out how much the tax would be and fumed about that additional expense.

The lesson learned was to "Stick with it…be tough… don't compromise when it is important." Decades later, I still have the Corvette to remind me that not all education is gained in school.

The Thespian

"...Oh, it's an actor's life for me!"
—*Pinocchio*

Another disruption came when I decided to move from the family home. I was an adult, with a job, and I wanted a taste of freedom and my own space. It was unheard of in a traditional Italian household for a "child", of any age, to leave the nest except to get married...and sometimes not even then. But I persisted, and found a congenial friend to share the expenses of an apartment. Once again Dad and I were at odds, as we were for much of my life.

Dad, as usual, was hard-headed and set against the plan...dictating that if I moved out I must thereafter knock on the door when I came home...no more walking in as if I were part of the family who lived there. Dad would never visit any of my apartments...although my mother often visited and even helped to furnish them.

My older brother Maurice, thinking to help the situation, told Dad that my buddy and new roommate, Angelo, was a respected thespian and teacher. Thanks, Big Brother... this was not the kind of help I needed.

Weeks later, when I returned home for a family meal, Dad uneasily, took me aside. "Francis, what went wrong? Why are you like this? How come you live with a guy? Maurice tells me your pal Angelo is a lesbian...why?" Dad really thought he had done something wrong in my upbringing. The relief on his face was almost comic when I explained the difference between a thespian and a lesbian.... and that I was neither.

Once the air was cleared, Angelo became close to Dad. He felt a connection with him. His own father had died when he was young and my dad was the epitome of a traditional, strong and somewhat detached Italian father.

"Work in the Food Industry and Never Be Hungry."

—Dad

At Dad's age of 55, he and Mom realized a dream by opening their own restaurant in Endicott. They had worked as a catering team for more than 25 years waiting for this opportunity. Dad cooked from "scratch", not just great Italian dishes but food from other nationalities as well.

Interestingly, Mom was the only one who cooked for the family…keeping the traditional Italian "sauce" simmering on the home fires. There was a clear division of labor. Although Dad had washed dishes in the CCC, he certainly never did at home.

Some Of Francesco's
Trade Secrets & Recipes

1.   To make a kitchen or home smell welcoming and appetizing, cut an onion in half and fry it on the stove.

2.   When preparing chicken, rub salt on each piece to clean and get the sliminess off the skin.

3.   Dandelion greens need to be dug up before the flower of the plant blooms. This ensures that the buds are very sweet.

4.   Pasta is a food for the soul. It comforts, strengthens…and a good dish of pasta is always remembered.

Minestra - any mixture. Cook Swiss chard chopped and boiled or steamed with large white beans or kidney beans, or navy or northern beans. Add rice. Mix this all together and season with olive oil and garlic (the flower of Italy). This dish can also be made with lentils instead of white beans.

Flower de Coogoots - soup or a side dish. Take the flower of the coogoots first thing in the morning and prepare a mixture of raw egg and spices and grated cheese. Egg and flour the flowers…get your olive oil hot…add chopped garlic.

Then place the flowers to cook...cover with cheese and coarse ground black pepper.

Probably the most important food in an Italian kitchen is the sauce. My friend, Angelo, tells a story about an experience he witnessed when Dad had a huge pot of scorched sauce at the restaurant...grounds for possible excommunication from the Sons Of Italy! Also, the restaurant operated on a slim profit and to discard that much sauce was not acceptable.

The pots were large and to start again would be expensive. Dad transferred the sauce to a new vat, then took a very clean piece of wood and dropped it in the sauce to simmer. It resembled a huge sausage bobbing in the tomatoes... after a time the wood was scooped out and the smoky burned taste was completely gone.

This experience made a deep impression on Angelo and, when that fateful day arrived when he, too, scorched a pot of homemade sauce, Angelo searched frantically for a magic chunk of clean wood...No wood!...until the creative Italian genius emerged.

Angelo grabbed a package of new wooden clothespins and dropped a dozen into the pot...after simmering.... Angelo carefully counted the clothespins as he removed them. Dad's alchemy had worked again with just a little ingenuity .

Another of Dad's variations for the burned sauce cure was to hold a piece of charred wood in the sauce until it pulled all the burn taste and acid out of the sauce.

The Dead Dance

Older people still stop me to reminisce about the wonderful meals Dad catered for their special events. Such memories are often brought up at what I refer to as the "Dead Dance".

In the early days of Italian immigration to Endicott, the men banded together to form the Independent Mutual Aid Society. Basically, it was an Italian insurance fund to pay the burial expenses of its members. Each year a dance was held as a fundraising project and social event. The amount dispensed to survivors at the death of a member is small, but the organization still exists.

Now, I, too, belong to the association and attend the dance...as respect for my heritage...and a way to keep in touch with the aging Italian community...people who are so important to my family.

Dad and Mom catered many of the Dead Dance parties... always serving his special pasta dishes...not an easy thing to do when all 300 attending were experts on Italian sauce.

Checchino and Cancer

"Illness can take away all but faith and heart."
—X. Fox

Dad worked in the restaurant for only five years and then was diagnosed with cancer for the first time. The cancer and his vulnerability to the disease surprised him. He was told death was a few months away. Dad stayed at home and fought the disease…becoming involved in caring for himself. He insisted on double chemotherapy, determined to live…and he did.

My mother, brother Maurice and his wife Dianne, and my sister Donamari kept the business popular and profitable for many years thereafter…but Dad never again cooked at his restaurant.

Live Now - Each Day - Don't Wait

"The web of our life is of a mingled yarn,
good and ill together."

—*Shakespeare*

In 1988 Mom died. The family had spent the day together at one of her periodic garage sales...one of Mom's favorite things to do. Dad called it "getting rid of her junks".

Later we proceeded to an Italian Festival and then went out to dinner...it was a great time. As we left my parents at home, Mom asked, "Will you be here for pasta dinner tomorrow?" It was a very out-of-character question, as I always showed up for Sunday dinner. Dad called later that evening and said he could not wake Mom up...she had fallen asleep in the chair watching TV...holding a framed photo of the family...and never awoke again.

"If there is a prayer to cover the situation of aging parents I would ask: Give me this day the ability to accept change as a natural part of life."

—S. Rose

"Everything Changes But Change."
—Zangwill

The first time I noticed a shifting relationship between Dad and me was about a year after Mom died. The progression was slow and at first only periodically evident...at least to me.

One particular evening Dad and I were alone as I drove him home. He began sharing his personal life with me. Dad with a personal life? Was I supposed to know this stuff...this was my father...who never mentioned sex to me. Not even "the birds and bees talk". Now he was telling me about his occasional lunches and dinners with women!

 Our discussions led Dad to ask what I thought about him being sociable. Since he was usually an introverted, private person, he was checking to see if it was acceptable to date and to respond to emotions.

At last, I started to listen; after all I am a trained therapist…. listening is what I was trained to do…but this was "Dad"...and it was a revelation to see the "man". I could hear the confusion and questions in his voice. "Is this okay, Francis? Is it okay to feel something for these women?" I listened, and at that moment Dad and I connected with a "real" discussion.

This was amazing....my dad...the man who had been the stern father...was a feeling, questioning, caring person. Mom had been his best friend and only close confidante... now he needed me.

I believe he had very few intimate friendships... Mom was his unwavering companion and when she was gone it was difficult to trust anyone else with personal information. As he shared his feelings with me he was also saying that he trusted me. Wow...the idea was overwhelming. At this point I just wanted to live up to the responsibility. Could I live up to it? This dilemma would evolve as we continued on our journey together.

As his guard and defenses went down, I began to see what must have always been there...a masculine gentleness.

Once the initial discomfort was bridged, and neither of us fell off the face of the earth, the personal discussions continued for many years. We were both still "real men" but now we could comfortably talk, and the interaction grew.

One time during our early ventures into the sex venue, Dad looked at me, smiled, and commented, "Ya know, sometimes it's like you're the father and I'm the son." Initially I was taken by surprise, but at last, I heard his need to be validated. "I'm glad to be here with you Dad...it's okay." We both recognized the evolving roles of the father & son relationship and knew that nothing more needed to be said.

Comfort with the social, emotional and sexual needs of aging is vital to a healthy aging process. Dad was always so modest as to his sexuality...it was an honor to be allowed into this very private area of his life.

I remember that many years ago Dad could play at being a verbal Romeo but, if a woman took him seriously, he would back off immediately. He could joke and even make some double-entendres, but all in fun. He enjoyed women; however, that was one menu he looked at but never ordered from.

"The Child is father of the Man."

—Wordsworth

Eventually, our relationship took an added depth. From being a son and advisor I was drawn into the role of consultant for finances, future planning and generally keeping track of whatever needed to be done

Dad had always been an integral part of my life. When I followed the family tradition and married a "good woman", although she was not Italian, Mom and Dad helped us obtain our first home. They didn't want grandchildren living in an apartment and gave us land on which to build. Dad went every day to watch the construction and added a bottle of champagne to be buried in the foundation.

As my own three boys were growing up, Dad was always available to drive them to games and appointments or just to spend time together. Our children loved being with him…he would tell them stories and make them laugh. Having Dad around with the boys was like having a warm glow around us all. The total acceptance of his grandchildren, just as they were, was beautiful to see. There was a deep bond between the generations…so much so that we often talk about Dad in the present tense.

Not that it was all sunlight and roses. Dad was not a warm and fuzzy guy. He was standoffish and often had his guard up. However, genuine warmth showed through for his grandchildren.

Sometimes, even with the boys there was an underlying tension regarding what the boys wanted and what Dad wanted for each of them.

All my sons had their own special relationship with him. Paul worked in Dad's garden. Brian at times kept a slight distance to be able to maintain his own personality....as did his brother Chris. Although the love was consistent.........there were so many generation differences.... the world was changing....and Grandpa had difficulty accepting he could no longer be the total boss of the entire family.

My sons learned early that their grandfather had a few immutable idiosyncrasies. One of these was his great distrust of railroad crossings. Whenever it was necessary to drive the boys somewhere, many extra minutes would have to be added... taking into consideration Dad would drive miles out of the way so he would not have to cross railroad tracks. The boys joked that to get from one side of Endicott to the other (a village of only 5 square miles) Dad would drive by way of Florida just to avoid the dangers of an RR crossing.

Eventually, changes in Dad's ability to drive became more apparent. I had known people, including clients in my psychotherapy practice, who had to deal with the problem of trying to restrict an impaired loved one from driving. It soon became necessary to limit the time our sons spent in the car with Dad...it was getting that bad.

It is such a fine line to walk, protecting the general population from slightly deranged drivers, against the rights and feelings of the deteriorating individual. We tried gently to let Dad know that he might be endangering himself as well as the lives and property of others. But, a driving license was a symbol of independence that he needed. Before we had to take a drastic action, such as confiscating the car, fate took a hand.

A serious accident brought the problem into focus for Dad. He dove to a nephew's house to visit one afternoon and, when leaving, put the car into reverse instead of into drive. He destroyed his nephew's front steps and porch and totalled the auto. Dad never drove again, although he kept his license. It was a matter of realizing just what he could still do, and what was no longer possible...but to a great extent the decision had to be his own.

A Gift for Fantasy

Perhaps because of the time he spent on a farm with his grandfather, Dad had a special connection with animals. His alley cat "Pepino" was a memorable pet. It behaved more like a dog...following Dad around... announcing visitors and eating spaghetti. That cat actually obeyed commands and was the hero in many of the stories Dad created for the boys as they were growing up. Often the stories were "fairy tales" from Dad's imagination... with an all-Italian cast of characters...the same versions he would tell when I was a child now became part of the next generation's heritage.

This tough Italian male had the essence of compassion in his soul that came through when dealing with all creatures. He had such a peaceful, quiet center. He attracted animals and charmed people just as easily. This may sound like a lot of contradictions, but it was really the same person. Dad, like all of us, was made up of many facets.

"The more serious the illness, the more important it is to fight back...mobilize your resources...spiritual... emotional...intellectual...physical."

—Norman Cousins - "Anatomy of an Illness"

We got used to Dad beating the odds. In 1974 he was diagnosed with cancer and told he had 6 months to live. He refused to believe it and lived another 25 years...a lot of life is faith and attitude.

When the cancer returned in 1995, I think the family assumed Dad would beat it once more and things would go on as usual. We hoped that death would wait again.

After Mom's death, his presence in our lives was even more significant. One of my sons asked, "Grandpa will be with us forever...won't he, Dad?" But this time the disease was relentless.

The Rubber Chicken

One of the realities of a dual-career family with children is that responsibilities have to be shared. My wife Helen's schedule was such that Thursdays were her long day at work. This meant for that evening I was in charge of dinner, homework enforcement and clean up.

Like a great many red-blooded American males, completing this series of events was a stretch for me. Not that I didn't know what to do; it just took so long to do it. Thinking up a menu, then cooking and clearing up was more time than I wanted to invest. So Thursdays became a night out to an inexpensive but good Italian restaurant. The return of cancer brought with it a gradual failing in my strong parent. We encouraged Dad to join the "boys night out to dinner" on Thursdays. Dad generally did come with Paul, Brian, Chris and me for spaghetti.

It was normal for a Battisti family outing at a restaurant to result in an animated discussion and review the service, menu choices and the food quality. Well, every week we would hear from Dad how the food just wasn't good enough. Either the pasta was cooked too long; the sauce was bitter or worse; sugar had been added.

One night I had what I considered a bright idea. Why not have Dad cook for us at his house on Thursday evenings? Initially he seemed hesitant but ultimately agreed to "do his thing" and show us how to prepare "real Italian food".

The boys were excited because they had never experienced Dad's cooking. Since Mom's death the large family meals at the family homestead had stopped.

I encouraged the cooking idea primarily because I was concerned with Dad's progressive retreat from the activities of life. I hoped the meals would spark his waning zest for life.

At last the big night arrived - the first Thursday dinner at Grandpa's. The menu was a traditional pasta and baked chicken. I was probably the one most excited because of the sensory memories of his fine cooking.

That night was a telling one...for the boys and for me...and for Dad. He had cooked enough pasta for three meager eaters...instead of three hungry teenagers and myself. Then came the turning point for all of us...the baked chicken. To say that it was overcooked would be a vast understatement. In fact, burned would be a kind description.

The boys were great...they ate...enjoyed...but knew there was a problem. Dad looked at me...puzzled...apologetic and striving for a shred of dignity. He said, "Maybe I'll cook it less next time...that darned stove never did work right."

We continued having Thursdays at Grandpa's. The meals got much better. Dad got back in the groove and I was reliving my memories and enjoying the Italian culinary delights. The boys even got into the act by creating salads.

This went on for two years and then Dad began having more and more difficulty navigating through kitchen duties. The master of the kitchen was no longer in control of his space. It was too complex to deal with food and cancer. Thursdays at Grandpa's stopped.

Thursdays were then filled with only occasional meals at restaurants and, toward the end of his time in his own home, we would bring carryout to Dad so we could all eat in the safety of his kitchen. It was a major change for all of us because it represented a supreme shift in nurturing.

Food, for Italians, as with many people, is a symbol of giving and love. We had passed from Dad nurturing us with his skill in the kitchen...to us giving to him from our hearts...still being together but in a different way.

One of the lessons life can teach is to pay attention to what is in front of us. So much time is spent running after something...goals...money...stuff...things we believe will bring us something, perhaps power or status or that elusive peace of mind. What we really need is to be present-oriented. People and relationships are what are important... be present and enjoy the moments with loved ones. I'm glad I could, at last, see that being with Dad was a fascinating and awe-inspiring experience.

The First Steps On The Last Mile

My sister married and moved to Pittsburgh, Pennsylvania. It was a very special occasion because Donamari had always been "Daddy's little girl", who, until the time of her marriage, lived at home with him. He was so proud walking her down the aisle; it was a milestone in both their lives.

After her move, I began to take on a larger role in Dad's care, although becoming a full time caregiver was a gradual, progressive process. Being in his own home was very important to Dad. Initially, as he needed more help, I would go to his house daily after I left work.

Doctor visits required scheduling and every detail of daily life had to be carefully checked. I would do the housework and yard maintenance that was getting too much for Dad…then check that he had taken the medications and set them up for the next day. Often he did not want to answer questions about eating or bathing. Perhaps he couldn't remember. He seemed embarrassed at not knowing details about his personal hygiene.

His memory was an important element in caring for Dad. I always felt fortunate because he and I could talk throughout his fight with cancer. I found it meaningful because this level of sharing and communication had not always existed between us. We learned so much about each other in those last few years. When Dad was so sick I put all the old feelings behind me…they were over. I accepted Dad as a person with all the strictness and limits. We learned to appreciate each other...at last.

Being a father myself was a great help in understanding my filial relationship. I don't believe my sons and I will have to wait that long...we work on having an open, committed relationship. The boys' assistance with the care for their grandfather brought us closer. Their experience with Dad gave them the feeling of being connected beyond themselves...and the value of life.

Theresa

"One night, as Old St. Peter slept,
He left the door of Heaven ajar,
When through an angel crept
And came down with a falling star."
—*David Baker*

We tried everything to help Dad maintain independence and remain living in his home. For a while, prepared meals were delivered daily. Dad complained the food was inedible and, after sampling a few of the dishes, I had to agree. Next we arranged daily visits by home care workers.

This was difficult for Dad to accept. He did not want a stranger invading his privacy...he was afraid they would steal...he considered the intrusion a security risk...no one was ever good enough to meet Dad's standards.

The right person arrived in the form of a volunteer. Theresa showed up to visit...and stayed to help Dad for over two years.

Theresa drove a Cadillac and Dad was impressed that he had worthy transportation. She drove him to medical appointments, took him out for lunch and often for dinner.

Other times they would just sit and talk for the afternoon. At last he felt seen and appreciated...he felt important. Theresa was a very special person who honored Dad and the rest of the family with her presence. The time she spent with him gave us all a sense of security...Theresa was our angel.

A "Wobbly" Memory

Having his cognitive functions reasonably sound seemed to offer more dignity to Dad by giving him a level of influence over his life. The intensity of my feelings about this issue crystallized during one of Dad's stays in the hospital. He occasionally became confused, thinking he was somewhere else. This is fairly common among older, frail people in the hospital. It was a concern but I felt it was a temporary condition.

As my wife Helen and I arranged for Dad's return home, one of the discharge planners registered surprise that he would be living alone. She asked if we were comfortable with that situation, considering his dementia. My reaction was anger. Dementia, what dementia?!

The planner agreed to recheck the charts and get back to us. It is so important for family or the caregiver to stay on top of all the treatments and options, medications and diagnoses. Just one incorrect entry on the data chart can cause a great deal of harm. With all the tribulation going on at this time, the needless worry of wrong information can be wearing on the patient and family.

Later, a call came that the planner had been incorrect. Even hinting at a dementia diagnosis had been a mother lode of fear for all of us.

I was annoyed for days. What if this eventually came true and we could not talk and laugh? I did not want to lose him that way. Oh how fortunate I was to have him now...today. I promised to savor each moment with

Dad…to not get caught up in the tasks and chores… to love our time together…to keep him safe, comfortable… and with us.

Before long that secure feeling about Dad's memory began to erode. He was getting things mixed up more often, confused about dates, and forgetting to eat. I would confront him about eating, and he would claim that he knew he had eaten. He would either smile at me or put his head down and protest that of course he knew he had lunch. I now know that in his mind he had eaten…and that was his reality. But he knew, on some level, that something did not feel right. Dad once admitted he thought his head was getting a "bit wobbly".

One evening I was driving Dad home in my new car. Realizing it was his first trip in the Pathfinder, I asked how he liked the vehicle. After a long pause, he answered very indirectly, by asking about the other car and if Helen was driving it now.

He had forgotten that Helen was in a very serious accident just a few weeks previously and that the car was destroyed. When I reminded Dad of the incident, he was upset and claimed that I had never mentioned it to him.

I nearly drove off the road. What was happening to my Dad? With great reluctance I admitted we could no longer overlook the possibility of dementia. Something was changing and we needed to deal with it.

He was tested and he did have mid range, short term memory loss. Fortunately there was no sign of dementia. But at last I knew…I was losing a little more of him each day. A lot of little things about his behavior fell into place.

It hurt…and I wondered if this was how it would be on the path we were following.

It was time to contact family members and let them know the details. Dad's inability to handle daily self-care was our primary concern in deciding where he would reside. Dementia is a major factor in the determination of appropriate housing for the elderly. We needed to discuss the adjustments and how to respond to his forgetfulness. Decisions had to be made for Dad…and for me. I needed to feel some control as my worst nightmare approached.

"Life is a succession of moments, to live each one is to succeed."

—*Corita Kent*

Dad was slowly deteriorating…in a rehabilitation unit in a long term care facility…recuperating from his seventh surgery in two years. We decided to have a traditional celebration for Fathers Day in 1999, although we put it off for a week so he could complete the physical therapy program.

Helen, our three boys, Paul, Brian, and Chris, Grandpa and I went to a restaurant as we had so many times before. This time we knew it was different…it was probably the last one with Dad…Grandpa…and we knew it…but did not want to accept the inevitable.

Dad was uncharacteristically quiet and it was noticeable to all of us. Usually he would have the boys laughing hysterically at his antics and stories…while I would be trying to keep us from getting thrown out of the restaurant for disorderly conduct. I thought perhaps he was beginning to disengage from life. As usual, I was looking for the clinical answer.

When the meal ended, Dad requested that I drive him back to the nursing home alone. This was strange as he always wanted one or more of the boys to ride along. We were driving for a few minutes when he looked over to me and summoned my attention. "Francis." Whenever I heard Dad call me Francis I knew something major was about to be said, and I had better be listening. He hesitated and then asked, "Do you think I have accomplished anything with my life?"

Wow! Was I ready for this discussion? The silence at the meal was not some brain failure or social isolation. He had been deep in thought. It was the integration of his life. What meaning had it held? My dad, broken English and all, was fulfilling the process of centuries...and now I was to be part of it. I, too, hesitated....well...(thinking, I'm a therapist, right? I can do this...) "What do you think Dad?"

"I think I have, Francis, I had a business, I was respected by people, I worked hard and I love God." That sounded good. He had been considering this for quite a while. Here sitting beside me, as we had so many times before, was my DAD, and he was amazing me with his capacity for insight. Why was I amazed? I guess I had been looking and only seeing Dad...not the man behind the person...beyond our relationship.

He also had not mentioned our family in his list of accomplishments and I wondered about this. I asked, "What about your family, Dad? You have always done the right thing for all of us." "That's just natural. A man always takes care of his family," he replied.

The lesson for me was that all humans are always thinking and processing. Perhaps not how I expected, but Dad was a thinker all his life and I never realized it. He had always been Dad. Now, it was important that I assist in reconciling the relevance and review of his life.

As we age, we all experience cognitive changes. Disease and circumstances have a direct impact on this level of functioning. However, the need to make sense of one's world is constant. Our search for integration of our life experience is natural and innate. There comes a time for review and reflection on life…in Dad's case, a "life well spent".

In these final days, before my eyes, Dad often exposed his life. It was a gift, a moment in time I will always treasure. As caregivers we need to assist and encourage this process…if we can…if not, don't judge…and don't get in the way.

Peace In Unexpected Places

We tried to continue our lives as usual as possible so I attended an annual International Creativity conference. Helen called this "a week at camp for Fran".

During one late afternoon meeting I was feeling disjointed, lonely, and sad....a familiar experience at this convention. As part of the discussions, our feelings were examined, validated and explored in relation to "real life".

Just prior to this interlude I had been involved in a workshop where I discussed the failing health of my dad.

I was lost in thought when suddenly I became aware that I was strangely relaxed. A comfortable, homey and secure aura surrounded me. It was so strange because I had not felt this secure in many years.

As I became more aware of my surroundings...what was causing my mind to ignite with peace was listening to a discussion of fellow conference attendees...speaking in Italian.

I continued to sit alone and just listen to the musical sounds of the familiar words. I appreciated the tone and vitality without understanding the meaning. I listened as I had many years before...when my family would visit the paesani on Sundays. The language was a connection to heritage, family...and Dad.

Occasionally, life is like origami...a constant folding and re-folding of experiences...what we do with each movement in time impacts on the next...building a life... remembering and moving forward.

As an interesting aside, it never occurred to me when I was very young that Dad's speech had an Italian accent...it was just part of who he was.

Evolution Of A Relationship

The changes continued, not just the father/son relationship, but rather a change of need and control. For me, the added dimension of also being a father of three young males added to the zest of the mixture. Much has been written about the concept of the "sandwich generation", and I was having an internship in it. There is a profound difference between theory and life.

As the cancer spread, Dad's health became more compromised and the hospitalizations increased. We started to realize that he needed rehabilitation services immediately following this latest hospital stay. If he was going to continue living on his own he needed the extra time to develop strength. "Living on his own" was a metaphor for being in charge of his life, although he had long ceased to be able to function alone. Our desire, and his, was for him to live in the family home for as long as possible. This was a desire that took extensive coordination, cooperation and continual discussion. It was important to meet his needs and give Dad some input on the future...he had such a waning grasp on any control of his life.

Rehabilitation Home

When searching for a suitable temporary rehabilitation home I looked for what I envisioned as an ideal setting. Having been familiar with many of the long term care homes in the area, I was pleased that Dad would be residing in one I knew well and liked. I knew the staff and had consulted at this facility for ten years.

I thought, perhaps, he would enjoy the community of living in the rehab unit and that he might decide to continue residing there. Everyone has their own agenda in these situations. The key is to be aware and prioritize. At this point, Dad's focus was primary.

The administrative process of hospital discharge and entry into a long-term care facility is enough to age anyone. At best it can be described as a morass of forms that have little to do with anything of interest to the patient or family.

As with most of life, bureaucrats were in charge of designing the system which meant neither caregiving nor assisting nature was a priority. This frustration was shared by the facility personnel who had to abide by the dictates of a highly regulated health care system.

Another rule with ambiguities is the need to be transported from the hospital to the care facility via ambulette. Dad was not happy about this, but, realizing it was demanded by "policies", he agreed. He stated, however, "Medicare better pay for this because I didn't want the ride in the first place." Interestingly, although the ambulette is required for insurance purposes, Medicare does not cover the cost…and the family pays.

Being with Dad, or any cared-for individual at the time of transfer to a care facility, is crucial….so there is no sense of abandonment. The process is daunting and lengthy and it contributes to confusion no matter how much family and management try to make it otherwise.

Entering the facility, Dad was met at the door by the administrator who was outside smoking. Dad thought the "boss" was at the door just to greet a Battisti to the home. This was momentous because Dad believed he was really welcome…he was seen and was still important. The man had a very Italian name. Dad observed, "Hey, this guy is Italian!" I replied, "Dad they are all Italian here." Dad laughed, making a smooth transition possible. Later, when friends or family would visit, Dad often mentioned that he was personally met at the door by the number one man at the home. I never did tell Dad that it was just a fortuitous accident.

Then, more paperwork. It is important that the patient be involved in this, depending on physical and cognitive resources. If more appropriate, the individual can be updated at a later time. This helps the cared-for person maintain as much autonomy and dignity as possible. Being involved in decisions is self-empowering.

Admitting Dad to the facility went fairly well. The staff was attentive, knowledgeable and concerned. Dad requested a private room, which he received, but he did not like being unable to lock his door. House rules….the doors cannot be locked from the inside in any long term care facility.

"Why not, whose room is this anyway? Who is the boss here?" Dad complained. Well, I made light of the open door rule and it was a mistake that would come back to bite me later.

Realizing the power of regulations, at the same time I forgot the power of Dad's mind-set once he felt strongly about a subject. He did not feel safe and in control of his environment...negating cardinal rules for a smooth transition into care facility living.

I knew control was very important to Dad. This temporary arrangement was an acceleration of the change process in our relationship. Was I being too dominant? Could Dad tell that I was relieved with this arrangement? Truthfully, I did sleep like a baby that first night, mostly because I did not have to agonize about his safety.

I had not realized how much effort and stress were building up with the constant care for Dad in his own home. But, now I did not have to worry that he was alone. The time Helen, the boys and I had spent each day caring for his home, meals and personal care could now be spent in other ways.

I stayed most of the day at the facility with Dad meeting the staff. Everything was fine that first night until I got to the parking lot and the privacy and security of my car, out of the eyesight of the staff.

Then it hit me...I cried vigorously...abandonment of Dad...the deteriorating nature of his health...the cancer was in command. Then...the guilt....the responsibility. Although intellectually I knew this was a normal response, rationality went out the window. How could I do this to him? I was being a bad, self-absorbed son. Did Dad really need this placement. Who was this respite really for? I'm glad I did not have to make the health proxy decision at this time. My stomach hurt...maybe it was hunger...probably not. The hunger was for relief...hunger for Dad to be well again.

I thought at the time, "This is so hard. I need to cope now and do what is necessary...later I will release the feelings....now we 'do'."

At a time like this a personal support system is crucial. My wife, Helen, was there for me when I got home....reaffirming that, no, I was not the worst person to set foot on the planet; and yes, Dad really did need to be where he could get strong enough to return home.

Also, we had to admit that the placement was for Dad and myself. I needed...we needed...some rehab time. Care-giving impacts the entire family. No matter what I was doing or who I was with, throughout the day I was always aware of Dad's increased vulnerability and my increased responsibility for him. I am my father's keeper.

My son Paul was with me during some of the worst decisions and his presence was so helpful. Even through his own sadness that his grandfather would not know the next generation of children in our family, Paul was a great comfort to me.

As my relationship with Paul, Brian and Chris evolves, we all realize they may be making decisions for me or their mother one day. Each one has said he would do so gladly, as there is no limit on love, and care just comes with the package. Wow…again the voice of time brings connections with the generations.

A Smoking Statement

The relationship transition between Dad and me became very evident with a call from the long term care home about a week after Dad's admission.

The voice on the phone was familiar; a person I had worked with previously. She was initially hesitant and then informed me that Dad, my Dad who had enforced rules in our home diligently and with immediate due-process, was found smoking a cigar in his bathroom...a definite fire hazard and definitely against the rules.

Was this the care facility calling or one of my sons' schools calling to report unacceptable behavior? This was the epitome of the sandwich generation. Was Dad going to get "in-home suspension"? Or would he be sentenced to write on a blackboard, "I will not smoke in the bathroom ever again?" Here it was, his "Who's the boss here anyway?" attitude. Now, how do I handle this?

Later that day when I was visiting with Dad, he completely denied the incident. First, he said they were making a big thing out of it; then the denial; then, it was the gentleman down the hall who was smoking and the smoke just happened to come into Dad's bathroom. Well, whatever the cause, I could hear Dad's embarrassment and demand for control...some control...any control.

Too many times we look at the behavior and are blind to the motivation. Dad was holding on to a last shred of dignity, trying to impose his will. Rather than fight him we should have joined him in his struggle...or let him know we recognized the importance of the need to assert his rights as a man still involved in life.

The care facility can be commended for looking at this issue for a resolution that was centered on meeting the need of the patient first and not the old policies of adhering only to the "medical model approach".

They looked for an alternative solution to meet the need of both resident and residence...respecting the "individual".

Balancing Dad's desire to smoke and his need for rehabilitation and the facility's desire for safety, it was decided he would leave all matches at the nurses station. When he desired to smoke he would pick up, not ask for, his matches and get assistance to the smokers room. I also needed to let all the family know of this agreement, lest they object, not realizing the true significance of the decision.

We again needed a family council to decide on living conditions. Dad could no longer live alone. The doctor advised there would be no further need for rehabilitating care. Death was in the near future for Frank Battisti. At this time we decided that Dad would live with us for as long as possible.

Give me the strength to recognize death as the natural response to the summons of nature.

—X. Fox

Somewhere along the eons the paradigm for death changed. Death is no longer an accepted, integral part of life but a vile enemy to be delayed at all cost. Death and cemeteries are feared...as if the dust of a burying ground could cling to shoes and unwittingly shuffle one closer to death.

As the life span lengthens, more people are reaching an age where some level of care is necessary. Long ago it was expected that the generations live together and care for the elderly until death. It was part of the normal progression of generations. Death was a natural order of life and not the black cloud of fear many people today try to defy or deny. Modern medicine has led us to expect recovery...to live through events and diseases that a few decades ago would have been fatal.

Death is the bill of nature that cannot be fought. Life does end...sometimes unexpectedly. When death is a prolonged process due to illness or age, the dynamics change. There are no absolute answers and guilt at some level is almost a given, but it is mitigated through knowing you did your best. (Although it is very difficult for someone of Italian heritage not to feel guilty.) We must give life the significance it deserves by allowing death dignity.

When we accept deep within ourselves the fact that we all will die, that our days are numbered...then we become more fully alive as vital individuals.

Home At Last - A Last Home

"Home is where you are happy."
—Henry Anatole Grunwald

So much has changed...children...siblings often live hundreds of miles away from parents and home care for the ill or elderly is often no longer possible...but for me it was possible. It was a privilege to participate closely in the last months of Dad's life.

I know some people who have chosen a long term care facility for their loved one, and others who have chosen to pay for help to let the care receiver stay at their own home for as long as possible. Bottom line? There are no wrong choices...just difficult ones.

Care for Dad in our home was a major commitment. Helen made the transition feasible. We turned the living room into a care unit. I had planned a sabbatical from work for six months to travel and study in England. However, Dad's deteriorating health and the health of Helen's mother made the trip impossible. I spent much of this time at home, just being with Dad. Helen said we were "blessed to be able to walk with our parents during their last days." But I still had mixed feelings about accepting the inevitable or fighting the disease to the end.

And, here again, is a fine distinction. We could no longer focus on doing for Dad; it was important for us to be with him. Let me always be generous with time; it is the true coin of existence. On the approach to eternity we need to walk with the dying and no longer resist destiny.

"The power of thought,...the magic of the mind!!"

—Byron

❧ Breaking the news to Dad was difficult at best. When I explained that we wanted him to live with us for the duration he hesitated...and asked if it would make a difference if he gave up his cigars...a bargaining chip to live longer. This was the moment for me to let go and give him the power of choice.

When Dad developed cancer twenty-five years earlier he stopped smoking cigarettes...the potent old "Lucky Strike" brand. As the years passed he started to smoke cigars, "but not inhale." He said when he had a cigar he felt like "a big shot". I battled with him for years to stop and even tried rationing the cigars. Ultimately, I realized it was his right to smoke. Now, I just wanted to be with him and not hold on to the old conflict.

He eventually agreed that he wished to be with us to the end. Respect is an Italian mantra and not just a cliché. With that degree of regard for each other, we could handle anything.

Before settling into our home, Dad requested a last visit to his own house. He walked in and sat in his favorite chair and said, "Okay Francis, you can leave now." I had to gently take his arm and insist, "Nice try, Dad, but let's go."

"Death gives life its fullest reality."

—Dalai Lama

The decision to call Hospice came after a lengthy discussion with a very informed doctor who was the medical director of the last facility Dad had been admitted into. I was so confused...the other doctors did not spell it out for me...and didn't make the decision easy. I had been thinking about housing options and this kindly man explained that there were very few options left for Dad... and Hospice was at the top of the list.

At this time of high emotional stress, Helen and I found our minds whirling and our need for clarity immense. We needed to remember that no one can do it all. We needed to graciously accept assistance from friends, family and organizations. We called Hospice.

Although other family members had concerns about bringing in Hospice, one call to the organization eliminated many of our fears. The reassuring, soothing voice on the phone gave us a sense of caring, understanding...and hope, although we still had many questions. How would Dad react to all these strangers? Would they only talk of death?

To our amazement and relief, the Hospice team brought with them a sense of peace, friendship and a deep desire to be with us in our grief. Whenever we had a question of pain management, or the process that Dad and the rest of us were experiencing, or the navigation of the medical system, Hospice was present with knowledge and reassurance.

The Hospice professionals and volunteers allowed us

all a level of comfort during Dad's final days. The palliative care approach considered all of him...mind, body and soul. This included the right to die with peace and dignity, free from avoidable distress.

Rather than keeping the person alive at all costs, the emphasis is on the relief of pain and other physical symptoms, and addressing the individual's entire emotional needs.

As Dr. Elizabeth Kubler-Ross stated: "Those who have the strength and the love to sit with a dying patient in a silence that goes beyond words will know that this moment is neither frightening nor painful, but a peaceful cessation of the functioning of the body." Hospice on a regular basis helped us gain that strength and love.

As I look back, it is clear that I encouraged and pushed Dad to maintain his independence...because the struggle was mine. He wanted to sit comfortably and I wanted him to keep himself moving. I just wanted to keep him with us for a while longer. But at a certain point it was no longer about keeping Dad healthy physically. That part of the equation was over. What we all needed was peace until his impending departure. One day I fought death... the next I accepted the inevitable.

What Dad's experience taught me is that sometimes a person needs to let go in order to move forward. The struggles and needs of life change almost without our knowing...but Dad knew what he needed. The care-giver's needs are secondary, no matter how much we think we know better. We must let the dying lead the way through the twilight phase of their existence.

We did not know exactly how much time was left with Dad, so Hospice encouraged us to do and say anything we needed. Humor was once again present in our home. Life is for the living and Dad was still living.

"It is relevant not that the person is dying, but that they have lived."

—Anonymous

Dad and I spent time together that was great, when we could forget the eventual parting. I loved the moments we would sit on the deck and talk. He would speak of how much he missed his "Se", his affectionate name for Mom, Sylvia, and how much he was looking forward to seeing her when he went to Heaven.

Sometimes I would cut his hair and his nails. The hair cutting was a very intimate process for both of us. My mother always would cut our hair; initially it was to save money. I found it to be very nurturing. I checked with my dad and he felt the same way. Now we had this to share.

Another time we discussed his early life in Italy under the Fascist dictatorship. His opinion of Mussolini was that "…he made the trains move on time, but got mixed up with the wrong crowd."

Once Dad got to America his attitude changed. He said, "Under a dictator you do what you are told. I believed that Italy was the strongest country in the world…that we had it all. When I came to the United States I was so surprised to see all that was here. I then realized how my faith in the dictator was betrayed and how powerful his brainwashing could be."

"Mankind must remember that peace is not God's gift to his creatures; peace is our gift to each other."

—Nobel Lecture - Dec. 1986

Dad loved to watch TV...the Yankees, westerns, cooking shows...adventures...what else does an 85-year-old need? One night I was at the computer when I had an insight...here I was living my life at a normal pace...home in the evening...taking time off from my practice just to be with Dad. His circumstances had dictated that we all live our lives calmly and with balance.

As his life was on the final journey, we were learning that internal calmness offers external clarity. We had seen the cancer as the enemy, but it also gave us a reason to take the time to express our feelings...our love...to step beyond the fear and open our hearts.

We all give differently depending on circumstances, time and our emotional connection to the dying. I realized that, if I was constantly moving and doing, I would never enjoy the inner realm of being. Dad reached this central calmness. He moved toward the light.

"RESOLVE to be tender with the young, compassionate with the aged, sympathetic with the striving and tolerant with the weak and wrong...because sometime in your life you will have been all of these."

—Anonymous

꧁ The special relationship Grandpa had with the boys also went through changes. He went from the bastion of calm reserve and self reliance to one of need and frailty. On both sides the situation was handled with dignity.

The boys performed very personal care for their grandfather. At first they were hesitant and a bit scared, but eventually they did it gladly...still eager to spend time with him...and to help. It gave them a good feeling to be able to assist in making his life more comfortable. And yet, Dad was still worried about everyone else...wanting to take care of them until the very end of his life.

By August of that year, Dad's health was steadily deteriorating. He wanted to stay in bed more and more often. He seemed to feel safe in the confines of his bed.

Even his smoking of cigars started to slow down. Those villainous cigars probably caused much of the advancement of his cancer. Although I called cigars killers, in Dad's opinion his cigar was the most relaxing part of the day...and was something he thoroughly enjoyed. We had argued so many times over his smoking, but now cigars had lost their appeal to Dad.

"Let me cope with intimate care with kindness and patience."

—S. Rose

I remember a time early in our changing relationship where the lines blurred. When Dad was still living in his own home he fell on the ice-covered steps. I didn't know about the fall until a few days later when I watched him move with a bit more difficulty. He said his back was a little sore…but nothing major.

Cautiously, somewhat hesitant and embarrassed, I requested a look at the damaged area. Good grief, be careful what you ask for. I quickly looked at his back, legs and, even more quickly, his derriere. Remember, this was my Dad…the head of the family…the man who made the ground shake. I was not ready for this shift in power…at least not this way. Fortunately, I did not find any physical problem that would need medical attention, but checking his butt cheeks would never be high on my list of things to do.

Both of us were ready to move beyond this episode. All too soon this experience paled in comparison to a greater need when Dad was living with us. I believe most of us will have the strength to give the care necessary by focusing on doing whatever is needed for the comfort of our loved one…one moment at a time.

I was still learning just what can be dealt with when necessary. This became very apparent when Dad was released from the hospital following an operation.

Previously, prior to leaving the hospital, I would arrange with the discharge planner for Dad to have a home health aide care for his most personal needs. Because of the type of procedure - bladder cancer - he was on a Foley catheter that the aide would change.

On this occasion I was out of town when Dad was discharged. Maurice and Dianne picked up Dad at the hospital but did not know about requesting an aide…and the hospital did not mention the service. When I returned later that day, 5:00p.m. on a Friday, I asked when the aide would arrive…and no one knew. So…I learned the basics of changing the Foley that weekend. I wasn't sure if my dad and I would get through this…but we did…we had to. Sometimes fate makes the decisions.

Then, after Dad moved in with us, his right foot developed a deep sore that hurt when any pressure was placed on it. The Hospice nurse changed the dressing daily and I fulfilled the duty on weekends.

I never believed I could be comfortable changing a major dressing like this one. It still impresses me how much a person can adjust when a loved one is in need.

Men should have a voice in caregiving. They have a lot to offer the elderly and dying. More men need to know that it is okay to care deeply…to feel and express emotions. Men can offer knowledge, strength and power to a situation from their perspective.

Love is the strength that gets us through intimate care and the needs of a body in decline.

Farewell

"And we will trust in God to see thee yet again…"
—*Bryant*

In September I went back to teaching at the college and Dad's days continued to be unpredictably predictable. We knew each day his health would worsen but we prayed for it to get better. We couldn't entirely give up hope.

Family and friends came to visit often and this was a healing for Dad…for all of us…it was a time to say goodbye. Their attention and offers of comfort were part of our support system. This connection to others and our moments together made the reality of parting easier to bear.

That autumn there were special times getting Dad ready for bed at night. We took care of ordinary tasks of changing the bed, medications and denture cleaning. And an important part in care…touching… a pat on the arm…a hug… just to let him know he was not alone.

I would on occasion give him a back rub. He admitted no one had done so since Mom died eight years ago…and it made him feel more alive. I believe this physical communication can lessen a feeling of isolation…and serve as a reminder that the person is still part of the family or community.

After chores were done, I would bring Dad his mother's crucifix. It had been given to him by his mother just before he left Italy. He would kiss the stigmata and say a prayer. Witnessing this was being present at a very special spiritual ceremony. It was peaceful and at the same time powerful. I felt so connected with Dad, God and the generations before me.

Part of this ceremony was the opportunity to sit on Dad's bed and talk with him for a while. We felt close to each other in these moments of sunset. In some ways these talks were a highlight of my life...except for the dying part. At the time I wished that we had talked throughout our lives together...but it was never so.

I think that as men, even though father and son, there was just too much at stake for us to communicate so intimately...but now it was the need to give freely of our love that released the words.

As Dad got closer to death he was dreaming of his mother more often. He believed he would be reunited with her...and enjoyed talking about her. The stories of family were his processing and putting a sense of integration to his life....getting his thoughts together for the last journey.

One night in particular we had a conversation that nearly choked me up...again. He mentioned several times that perhaps he should move back to the nursing home. I was surprised and not sure what he really meant. He would usually say this when he was uncomfortable or in pain. Again...what was going on? Were we not caring for him properly?

Helen had the insight to see that he might be saying he was too much trouble for us. She was so good at helping me to keep a balance in life. I pursued this idea with him the next day by starting our conversation telling him how much we enjoyed having him with us in our home.

I then asked about his statements concerning the nursing home and asked if he felt he was too much care for the family. He asked if he was a problem. Holding him and rubbing his arm, I told him again how much this time meant to all of us…and how much we loved being with him. I explained that our home was full of joy with his presence. He stayed up late that night and ate very well…he was truly home.

Helen has been a courageous part of this process. Her mother died of cancer just seven months before Dad. Although the circumstances were different, she was as prepared as anyone can be for taking care of a loved one at the end of life.

Smell and color are some of the last senses to leave the elderly, so preparing food that looks tempting is important. Helen is working on her Ph.D. in nutrition so her background and advice were invaluable…even a puree can be colorful.

"…Make me always ready, to come to you with clean hands and straight eyes…so when life fades, as the fading sunset, my spirit may come to you without shame."

—*Native American prayer*

There are so many end-of-life issues to deal with. The caregiver must set aside guilt, anger and fear to make the concluding moments of life an expression of love…for it is a privilege to accompany someone to the threshold of destiny. The whole family, and especially Dad and I, learned to relax and enjoy each other. Even in the shadow of death we had the beauty of togetherness.

At the end Dad knew he was not dying invisible or alone. Friends and family were near and he was present in life. The dying need to remain integrated in the community of care. As long as there is breath in the body a person needs to absorb time and experiences.

The legacy of Frank Battisti's struggle adds meaning to my life's work. We should all be mindful throughout life to truly see, to truly know our loved ones. I spent my entire life with Dad but still learned more from him and about him as he approached death.

The specter of death offers us an opportunity to grow, gain meaning and purpose in our lives. The eternal quest for life in the shadow of death also adds pain, heartache, some knowledge, and perhaps, contentment. All lessons necessary for the living.

If you agree to care for an ill or elderly loved one, it

can be a very long road…and others in the family will always have questions about your decisions. I got my share of pressure from a few people about the choices I made…but never from Dad.

Do not expect accolades for shouldering the responsibility of caregiving…your reward is the peace of having given your best. The saddest words are…if only.

Sometimes our days together were tender beyond reason…and at other times my blood pressure would be noticeably higher than normal…a physical response to emotional overload.

Everything was so difficult for Dad toward the end. Every move was an effort but he kept his sense of humor. More and more we depended on Hospice to maintain their presence with us…for physical assistance…for advice…. for comfort.

"Give me this day...the ability to handle the practical matters...to discuss the arrangements with my loved one...Life and death are only separated by a moment."

—*X. Fox*

Dad and I also needed to discuss practical matters. He was quite open, saying, "I don't want to go, don't want to die, but we can't control death. Just no pain please." We tried to adhere to his wishes and desires.

The next considerations were making sure his will expressed his wishes. A living will is probably one of the most important documents any of us can execute. Also, we made sure that the health care proxy was current and in effect, and that funeral arrangements and all other legal aspects were in order. All are matters that should be taken care of long before the necessity arises.

The volunteers and professionals from Hospice continued to be with us, allowing the closing of Dad's earthly existence to be one of living, caring and dying with dignity.

The palliative view of death and dying regards the process as natural and personal. The goal is to provide the best quality of life to the very end of life. The patient's preferences and choices are adhered to at all times while still acknowledging the caregiver's concerns.

"Grant me the wisdom to know when to say goodbye...it's all right...go in peace. At times there is a fitness to the approach of death."

—*S. Rose*

Death is the dawn of eternity. On a Sunday afternoon, with family members at his side and his faithful companions the family dogs close by, on September 21, 1999, with anticipation and relief, with pain and grief in our hearts, Dad's work on earth expired. His circle of life was complete.

His last words to me were: "I'll be there when you get to heaven..." We agreed that I would be with him when he left, and he would be there when I arrived, hopefully at the same destination.

A priest, who was also a family friend, was called and arrived to spend these precious moments with us.

Hospice arrived immediately to share in this time of great transition. These people are beacons of light guiding a family through despair with the grace of a caring community.

Surprisingly, Dad had some specific ideas about his funeral and had been very willing to discuss the proceedings. All his life he was not a flashy person. But at his wake he wanted a band...live music at the funeral and the musicians accompanying the casket from the funeral home to the burial grounds.

Hmmmm...I was not familiar with any funeral practice like this. So I talked to the priest and a music director.

Although it was not feasible for the band to walk the long distance to the cemetery, we did arrange for a memorable wake. Dad wanted the funeral to be about life...not the moment that separates the living from the dead.

The music and gathering at the funeral home were exactly what he wanted. The three-piece ensemble played quiet, reflective melodies and a few Italian tunes. There were three viewings. Friends and family came back a second time to show respect, camaraderie, and appreciation for the music. At the final viewing and closing of the casket, the band played "Arrivederci Roma"....and the tears flowed.

During Dad's last days, the staff and volunteers of Hospice were with us...as well as during the funeral and afterward. They helped us compassionately, allowing death to approach with dignity. We savored Dad's days of life, even through the agonies of a prolonged demise.

A week after the funeral a beautiful basket arrived full of Italian delicacies. The Hospice staff was still with us...and would continue to be. Hospice is not just for the dying, but for the whole family. All life is precious, and all life...to the very end...deserves to be honored.

An 1848 tombstone epithet reads: "We loved him." There is no greater accolade than to be loved unto death.

PART II

Be Prepared

"All of life is a learning experience that extends through the last moments of the final journey."

—*X. Fox*

In religious tradition, dying and being reborn is an integral part of faith. Although modern culture and scientific progress have made some challenges to the march of death…it is inescapable. Through my own experiences, I have come to believe that death and the caregiving ordeal are actually life affirming…everything is put into perspective.

No one can truly be completely prepared to deal with the pain of loss through death. However, some of the distress can be mitigated by realizing you are not alone… others have survived the process and are willing to share their knowledge

My advice? I would say start preparing for the future now. Communicate with your friends and family about their wishes regarding long term care…and voice your own preferences. Make these desires legal and put everything in writing. Don't think you have a long time to consider the options. This becomes your issue sooner than you think.

As the life of the person you are caring for is ending, consider provisions for your own demise. It is a classic case of, "Speak now or forever hold your peace."…and forever could be right around the corner. If you do not prepare legally…you have lost your last chance…someone, or some institution or a government agency will intervene and make those decisions in your stead.

My dad always wanted to write a humorous book about cooking. He was a chef who envisioned both cooking and art as the process of giving something of oneself so others could be nurtured. This book is not about cooking, but I hope by sharing our stories, memories and the understanding we gained, it will be of benefit to those on a similar path.

Dad is writing this with me…by offering the opportunity to share his life and death so I could learn and impart this knowledge to others. Perhaps my words will ease your own way through this passage in time.

"Caregiving is an ode to the human spirit...to the capacity to love...to the ability to cope with the aging process...and death."

—S. Rose

The ancient double-faced Roman mythology symbol of Janus represents the past and future of life....and the faces of change. It is the twin process of caring for an aging loved one as both move toward destiny...and their separate journeys become one.

Janus is also the god of portals and beginnings. Caregiving is a season of growth, learning, and accepting the opportunity for life enhancement....for both the caregiver and the receiver.

The dynamics of caregiving changed significantly over the years. Today, almost ¼ of all households in America are involved in caring for an aging family member or friend. Nearly 80% of the caregivers are women who have spent years caring for children and are now caring for elderly parents.

The new reality of life often means being part of the sandwich generation...caring for both children and elderly family at the same time. Interpreted as...your emotions are being squeezed from many directions.

The practice of long term caregiving is increasing in prominence as the population ages and life expectancy increases. This calls for attention to ethical and aesthetic considerations for facilities, for residents, and their families.

Also relevant is the fact that gerontological social work

is a rapidly expanding area of social work practice. A growing appreciation of ethical considerations, as they relate to aging issues, is occurring.

Individuals over 85 years of age constitute the fastest growing segment of the population. The combination of the growing number and proportion of elderly, as well as the application of costly health-related services for this group, has an enormous impact on the quality of life for all Americans.

Philosophy Of Transformations In Care

"When we transform nursing homes into communities,
places for living and growing, we will ultimately change
the very nature of aging in America."

*—Rose Marie Fagan, Executive Director of
the Pioneer Network, 2000*

There are several options to be considered when faced
with the need for long term care….and again there are no
wrong answers. It concerns where to find the most compe-
tent care to meet personal requirements.

Home care with assistance, home of caregiver, or
assisted living in a long - term care facility…all are acceptable methods of dealing appropriately with the needs of the
elderly or infirm.

While trying to find fair and equitable care, the costs
and the need for medical services must be considered. The
amounts have increased dramatically and the issue of ade-
quate health care has become center stage in our society.

For several years, I have participated in educating care
communities…drawing on an increasing awareness of the
need in this area and personal experience.

Long term care is evolving in the more enlightened
facilities. The environment is being designed with a home
atmosphere with the focus on the individual and not facili-
ty-centered care.   We are transforming institutions into
homes.

Some professional care organizations (formerly desig-
nated as nursing homes) have created a "campus of care"

consisting of cottages where several residents live in each unit in a family setting with a staff of caregivers. Other buildings contain residences for those in need of more advanced care, and facilities for full nursing care. This makes living into old age a more humane process. Each person is looked at as an individual in such residences.

Another demographic that was not previously addressed at care facilities is that the population consists of a high percentage of women - the concerns of men have not been a priority....this too is changing....as are the old guidelines ignoring the existence of senior sexuality.

Treatment patterns are adaptable to the resident, with the resident participating in all facets of a well-rounded lifestyle. Residents should be able to look forward to each day and to enjoying a stimulating atmosphere, interacting with other residents, staff, visitors and family. Ideally, residents should thrive in the home, not vegetate as often occurred in the past.

Care must be a sharing process, taking into consideration the wishes of the resident, relatives and the facility. The goal is to build a residential family, or community of care, involving interaction with outside schools, clubs and other groups. Also, pets and plants could be introduced into the facility...all to create a more relaxed setting...a welcoming, wellness environment.

Long term care can be structured to meet the needs of the person in creative ways, thus minimizing problems. Giving the resident choices...determination of daily schedules, washing, exercising, and a voice about meal contents and eating times all add greatly to a sense of independence.

We are talking about a revolution in thought…a new way of caring for and appreciating the elderly…a cultural new beginning. The changes demand a major commitment from participating facilities. The modifications are designed to maintain the dignity, safety and sense of freedom of each person. This builds a unique personal relationship between staff and residents…a partnership in life and care.

Respecting the individual is paramount. All old people are not the same. In fact, as we age we become more unlike each other because of individual experiences, desires and dreams. Our elderly should be considered valuable, independent components in society. Aging can be life-affirming, satisfying and meaningful…life can hold potential, hope and promise to the last breath.

While time fades youth, it also adds depth and wisdom…usually. Realistically, if a person is difficult through his early years, time will not automatically turn him gentle and sweet. But how we treat residents, wise or otherwise, should be determined with compassion and common sense.

Pride and dignity do not diminish with age unless we make the elderly feel less by dumping them into a cultural bone yard…in a holding pattern for death. These are the conditions I hope to help eliminate through education and inspiration.

Care Of The Caregiver

This complex thought is simple. As William Butler Yeats once wrote: "The journey internally is not only an important journey, it is the only journey." In caring for others, we need to allow ourselves balance and time to renew our own spirit.

The number of households involved in caregiving is expected to increase due to the increase in longevity. A "Fortune 200" article explained: "Extended life span does not mean people stay young longer. It means people stay old longer. The 'Golden Years' are lasting longer and losing a lot of their shining potential."

Caregiving is often thrust upon the family member who is geographically closest to the person needing care. Love and obligation are other factors in the decision. Someone needs to accept responsibility to assist the elderly with the necessary choices. It would be great if there were a group of family or friends to share the caregiving, but it often is one person who accepts the major obligation. It can be a fulfilling but stressful situation.

Caregivers in general do not get consistent help from family members, although family input is important. Illness can bring about reconciliation, healing and a realization of what is truly meaningful. We hope for that ideal, but perhaps it is improbable.

Don't expect an instant attitude change from everyone. Each person handles aging and death in their own way. Some people can't deal with the situation at all, but may be able to offer different types of support.

In my own case, my sister Donamari lived out of town and was suffering from multiple sclerosis. She was very emotional about not being in closer proximity to Dad and the rest of the family, but her frequent calls, e-mail messages and occasional visits were a great comfort.

We may not have all our family near physically when we need them, but in this era of modern technology most families can remain close through the phone and computers...they can always be near us.

My brother Maurice and wife Dianne would bring cheer to Dad by sharing his craving for junk food...often arriving with a breakfast sandwich for each of them...or indulging Dad with hamburgers and fries...why not?

Although Dianne spent time making home-made treats for Dad, I think his favorite was the salty, fat-filled, fast foods. They all enjoyed the time together and this too brought comfort and connection.

Depression is common in both the caregiver and the receiver. Over 49% of caregivers have experienced prolonged depression. Caregiving is an emotional roller coaster ride. Just remember, help is available...ask.

There is external and internal pressure in the care process along with doubt and worry. It is not wrong to feel this way...it just needs to be dealt with.

Tension is inevitable and it is not unusual to be overwhelmed. The gut speaks...at times the knot in my stomach...the lump in my throat and tears in my eyes were dominant...but I knew I had to go on...one step at a time...gathering the best of each day for tomorrow's memories.

This particular voyage through time is dappled with the unexpected. There are moments that vibrate with deep feelings and many others of monotony and melancholy. Ironically, all are intervals that define life.

Caregiving must be a balance of the needs and peace of mind for all generations involved in the extended care process.

For some of us, when the need arises, caregiving can become our purpose in life. It is a profound responsibility that demands we honor the needs of all involved.

Balancing this need with autonomy for the individual is a delicate process. The aging person should be assisted in making choices about where to live and the level of care that is required...not just told what is going to occur. It is imperative that the voice of the cared-for be heard.

At your home or in a professional facility the cared-for person should have a say in their meals, schedules, and social involvement....for as long as possible. All this, of course, is dependent on the cognitive functioning level of the individual. My dad was mentally with us for all the major decisions...and it should have eased the weight on my heart...but that was an unrealistic expectation.

Spending the last days of mortality with my dad freed me from my self-imposed, absolutely structured life. I found it possible to change, and learn. Life is what is important, not the "stuff" that clouds our vision of the truth.

Take advantage of therapy and respite time for caregivers. Remember, if the caregiver gets ill, burned out, depressed, sad, angry or runs away to escape...it will leave another need. All or some of these reactions are possibilities… and are common occurrences. The wish to escape to any destination is a normal consideration at times and should not promote guilt.

This is all part of the frustration package. The caregiver must deal with not being able to "fix everything" or do everything. Try to respect destiny and make passing easier for the one reaching the Final Portal.

Exercise, maintain a good diet, save some time for a few moments of quiet personal pursuits. Support groups are also a good venue for caregivers. Sharing makes the travails easier to bear. There is help in the community…take time to find it.

It is okay to be afraid. For most of us death is a voyage into the unknown and a long separation is inevitable. It is okay to show emotion. Grief and relief often mix with profound sorrow…but the living must live. There is life for the caregiver after the death of the loved one.

We are all headed in the same direction…how will you wish to be cared for?

"Life Is An Odyssey Of Learning To Deal With Change And Adapting To The Needs Wrought By Time."

—X. Fox

on the edge
battisti
N E T W O R K
of creating tomorrows

The Battisti Network is a highly regarded, multi-discipline consulting firm recognized as a premier provider of creative avenues for change initiatives.

Vision

To offer client/partner innovative approaches for creating an environment addressing individual, organizational, and community transformation.

Mission

To develop a close, interactive relationship with our client/ partners to assess their strategic objectives and develop unique, meaningful outcomes for meeting these objectives. Our activities are based on practical and scientifically researched applications that have evolved over thirty years.

Core Values:

Proactive-   being dynamic and innovative, creating opportunities for continuous improvement.

Caring-   offering services that place the clients' needs as the paramount focus

Integrity-   interacting to insure a sense of trust and ethical behavior.

Global Focus-   promoting the growth of the world community.

Health-   enhancing hope and self-efficacy.

Services and Networks

Speaking and Consulting

The Battisti Network speaks to corporate, not-for-profit and convention audiences, offering extensive consulting services to individuals and organizations in the areas of wellness, organizational/personal transformation and vital aging.

Retreats and Seminars

In order to allow participants creative avenues to explore, in greater depth, their personal and professional needs, the Battisti Network partners with organizations to offer retreats and seminars.

For information on services, please contact Francis Battisti at:

265 Main Street
Professional Building
Binghamton NewYork, 13905
www.battistinetwork.com
Email: battistiseminars@aol.com
Phone: 607-770-1355
Fax: 607-729-6203

FATHER & SON